MW00651447

Grand Cayman

To My dear friends

Lindsay Dern 3:16

Col: Ps. 40:3

Copyright ©1999 by Lindsay Terry

All rights reserved. No portion of this book may be reproduced in any form without the written consent of the publisher, with the exception of brief quotations in reviews.

Published by
FORWARD PUBLICATIONS
a division of Forward Leadership Resources
3526 Lakeview Parkway, Suite B-230
Rowlett, Texas 75088

Printed in Tokyo by
Toppan Printing Company America, Inc.
Los Angeles Office

Cover designed by
Dan L. Thompson, Thompson Design
Rowlett, Texas

Distributed in the Cayman Islands by
William H. Adam
HOBBIES AND BOOKS
P. O. Box 900 GT
Grand Cayman, Cayman Islands
British West Indies

The original slides of the 1952 photographs are owned and copyrighted by
Cayman Islands National Archive, Philip Pedley, Ph.D., Director.
The photographs are used in accordance with a contract
agreement between Lindsay Terry and the Archive.

Grand Cayman

Colourful Reflections of Yesteryear

by Lindsay Terry

with contributions by Bill Compton

The Impressions and Colour Photography
of an Early Visitor

Introduction by Captain Charles L. Kirkconnell, O.B.E. • **Foreword by Mark A. Panton**

FORWARD PUBLICATIONS
Rowlett, Texas
Dallas County

Dedication

To the wonderful people of Grand Cayman, who
in 1952 made us feel wanted as we lived among them.
They freely shared their hospitality with two young strangers from the
United States and let us participate in their daily activities as they revealed the
kind of caring, hard-working, proud
Caymanians they really are.

Acknowledgments

It would have been impossible to complete this book without the help and contributions of several other people and organizations.

Marilyn Terry, my wife, who helped in every area of the writing of the manuscript, compilation of the photographs and preparation of the total work for the printers.

Rebecca Terry, an outstanding court reporter whose expertise was helpful in preparing the manuscript. She is the wife of my our second son, Lance.

Bill Compton, who invited me to make the trip with him in 1952. I appreciate his valuable contributions to this book.

Starr Walker, my secretary, an excellent proofreader and typist.

Ruth Miller for proofreading and editing of the original manuscript.

John Gentsch, owner of FLASHBACK, in Dallas, Texas, who made valuable suggestions and who's company developed the computer files for all of the photographs.

Carole Kirkconnell, a citizen of Grand Cayman, who made corrections in the original manuscript and helped furnish facts and dates concerning Grand Cayman as it existed in 1952.

Captain Charles L. Kirkconnell, O.B.E., a Cayman citizen, who wrote the introduction and furnished valuable advice and information.

Mark Panton, a Cayman citizen, who wrote the foreword and who, along with his family, was a great encouragement during the 1952 visit.

Dan Thompson, graphic artist, who designed the cover and the jacket.

I express my appreciation to the many wonderful Cayman people who made the 1952 trip an adventure that will be remembered and cherished for a lifetime.

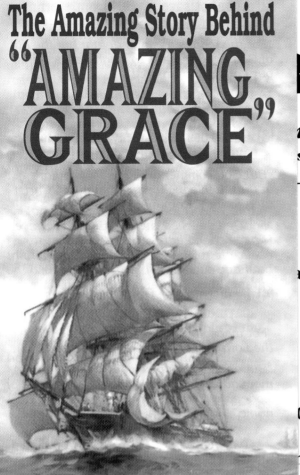

The Amazing Story Behind "AMAZING GRACE"

...and how it relates to you and me.

GRAND CAYMAN

Colourful Reflections of Yesteryear

Impressions and Colour Photography of an Early Visitor

Many of the colour photographs found throughout this book were taken in 1952 by Lindsay Terry, at that time a college student and by no means a professional photographer. His only photographic equipment was a small 35mm Kodak Pony camera. The photos, which were first developed as slides, were made into prints 40 years later, as you will see them in this volume. This collection is believed to be the most complete set of colour photographs made prior to the building of the first airstrip.

5

rial

vior,

long

sonal
ease
ill
elp

Foreword

When Lindsay Terry called to say he and Bill Compton would be visiting Cayman in July, 1998, he had to refresh my memory as to his identity. It had been 46 years since I had seen or heard from him. Lindsay said that he would like me to view some pictures that he had taken when he and Bill were here during the summer of 1952 and help identify people and places.

In the fall of 1952, I was planning to attend college in the United States and was concentrating on my dream of doing that. Getting ready to leave was no easy task in the early fifties. There were no

Mark Panton, in a 1952 photo.

government scholarships at that time for young Caymanians wanting a tertiary education. The picture that Lindsay took of my family and me at North Sound as I prepared to leave on the seaplane is priceless to me! You will see it as you look through the photos in this book. Bill, Lindsay and I left Cayman on the same seaplane at the conclusion of their visit. They returned to their college in Chattanooga, Tennessee, and I went on to Anderson, Indiana, to a college in that city.

My sister, Marion, was on the plane that crashed in North Sound three months earlier, and in the text they recall seeing the wreck when visiting North Sound. It must have caused them to think they should return by boat!

At that time I was a year younger than Bill and apart from a few short trips to Jamaica and Miami, I had not left home for an extended period of time. I thought it unusual that these two young men, near my age, would come to Cayman and stay for more than two months with no prior knowledge of our island or our people. I enjoyed knowing them while they were here. They witnessed the idyllic Grand Cayman that existed at that time and thought how lucky we were to live on such a beautiful unspoiled island! Yes, we had mosquitoes for a few months of the year, and there are many conveniences available today that we did not have, but there was a feeling of belonging to a caring community. We did believe that it "took a village to raise a family."

To see two adventurous young men from the U.S. in Cayman on a religious mission, with no means of support, was an inspiration to me and other young people. As I was to embark on a similar, but longer, adventure, their courage gave me hope. I am sure I asked them many questions about their city, state, and country. We enjoyed having them in our home, getting to know them and doing all we could do to make their time here pleasant. Caymanians competed to be hospitable to visitors and did all they could to make them feel welcome. After all, not many came to the "islands time forgot" in the early 50s. Our immigration department — mosquitoes — effectively kept the numbers low.

Since their initial evangelistic experiences in Cayman, Lindsay and Bill have been busy. They have led their lives and enjoyed their accomplishments in the United States as we have happily carried on our varied responsibilities here in Cayman.

I enjoyed seeing them again — some 47 years later — this time with their wives, and I regret not being able to spend more time with them. I welcome this pictorial montage of Cayman with the text giving impressions of life among us for the short period they were here. I think Lindsay captured it accurately. I am sure you will enjoy the colourful pictures which document a segment of our history and will be grateful they were shared with us.

Mark A. Panton
George Town, Grand Cayman

•

Mark is presently employed in the real estate business in Grand Cayman. Many members of the Panton family have for generations been influential in Cayman. He continues to live in the family home, a historic landmark building, in George Town.

Lindsay Terry, in a photo made by Silby Coe, Coe's Photo Service in George Town, Grand Cayman in 1952.

Preface

In July of 1994 my wife Marilyn and I, passengers in a Cayman Airways plane, were making our descent toward the modern runway on Grand Cayman in the Cayman Islands. My feelings and emotions were indescribable at the time. I was returning to Grand Cayman for the first time in 42 years.

As a nineteen-year-old college student of Tennessee Temple University in Chattanooga, Tennessee, I had accompanied Bill Compton, age 22 at the time, on a trip to the island, where I was to sing and direct the music in a series of religious services. He was to speak at those meetings. We had not been invited by any individual group or church but decided to go on our own and see what the outcome might be. We stayed two months and seven days, and the trip was one of the highlights of my entire life.

As I began this chronicle of our experiences, I was filled with excitement at the prospect of sharing with all who read this book the wonderful account of our visit. I looked forward to putting on paper my reflections and recollections of the people, the landscape, the food, the courtesies and all of the delights that contributed to our memorable venture.

The true purpose of the book is to share my reflections and the photographs of the island and her people as we found them, and as I remember them; therefore, I will not dwell on the religious aspects of the trip, such as describing the significance of the services, etc. There are, however, some notations of churches and their activities, because we found this to be an important factor in the life of most of the island people. Yet, I realize that people of many religious persuasions or no religious bent at all will be reading this book.

For those who may be interested in the message that we came to share with the Cayman people, it is very briefly discussed in Chapter 2 under "Church."

I want to share dozens of colour photographs that I took of people and places as they appeared prior to the building of the airstrip. The photos — slides originally — are the most complete set of colour pictures in existence, made prior to the building of the airstrip and the coming of tourism as they exist today.

I was surprised to see the lasting quality and colour of the slides made so many years ago with a small 35mm Kodak Pony camera. If a person would go to the exact spot where I stood as I made the pictures nearly five decades ago, he or she would see changes and advancements that truly are astounding.

It was not my intention to make this small volume an exhaustive historical account, although a brief history of the Cayman Islands is given. I am not qualified in the least to undertake such a task. However, if my reflections and the photos have some historical significance, then so be it. It is my understanding that there is a limited amount of written history of the islands.

Along with my thoughts and recollections, I would like to pass along to you in this preface a passage contained in a little promotional booklet which Bill Compton found in a folder filled with mementos and artifacts collected during our visit in 1952. It was written in 1937, printed in Scotland and contains quite a few black and white photographs. I am quoting this passage because it so perfectly pictures what Grand Cayman was like when we arrived. There is no way that I can portray it better.

Grand Cayman is a low-lying island composed of coral and coral-limestone. It is covered with dense, luxurious vegetation, ablaze with flowers, lilies of many varieties, orchids of amazing size and sweetness of smell, creepers, gorgeous flowering trees and shrubs. At eventide the air is full of delicate perfumes, and to lie on the beaches inhaling the gentle scents with the cool trade-wind fanning one, listening to the gentle lap of a sea coloured miraculously with the blues of every conceivable hue, is an experience not easily to be found elsewhere.

The photographs selected for this volume will reveal the beauty and perception outlined in the above quotation. There was a constant awareness on our part, even in our youth, of the natural beauty and grandeur of this Caribbean gem.

As the converted Navy PBY seaplane touched down on the shallow, reef-protected waters of North Sound in 1952, and as we were taken by boat to the shore to pass customs in a thatched-roof, one-room building, we realized that we were in a very unique place. We were not, however, aware just how unique until several days had passed during our visit. We encountered a warm-hearted, friendly people who welcomed us with open arms. They offered help at every turn, knowing that these "young men" would not be able to return the favors.

On the island we found a small world of rich history and a people filled with pride in their accomplishments with a deep-seated passion to make their island a better place. It was apparent that they enjoyed answering our questions concerning their island. Little did they realize that the heart of their beloved George Town, with an occasional car and not a foot of paved roads, would in just a short number of years be well on her way to becoming a thriving city, filled with tourists, taxis, rental cars, hotels, and hundreds of banks and businesses. Although conveniences such as transportation, electricity, telephones, and the means to fight a pesky mosquito problem were in short supply, the character of the people caused them to rise above their problems to build a life for themselves and their families that was both rewarding and happy.

It would not be long until the Old Courts Building, nestled near the seawall — quiet most of the time — would become one of the foremost attractions on the island. George Town Harbour (Hog Sty Bay), with its hand-built loading dock, suitable for smaller seaworthy vessels like the *Caymania* and the *Merco*, which came from Tampa, Florida, a couple of times each month, would soon be host to mammoth cruise ships from distant lands.

Little known at that time were the scuba diving sites waiting to be discovered and enjoyed by the thousands of visitors who daily marvel at the magnificent world of colourful marine life and their coral habitat just a few yards offshore. These underwater sites have inspired photography, the likes of which most of the world have never seen.

In the photographs you will see, among many other things, George Town landmarks such as the Town Hall, the famous Clock Tower, Elmslie Memorial Church, the Post Office, and the Old Courts Building — now the Cayman Islands National Museum — as they appeared in 1952, and as they appear today surrounded by the modern development that has become the new George Town.

When I returned in 1994, it was as if I had gone to a different place. Grand Cayman, as I knew it, no longer exists. Well...yes it does exist, but only in my heart and mind, and in my photographs.

I especially hope the older population of Grand Cayman will see the pictures, read my comments and recall the quiet, peaceful existence of yesteryear in their beautiful island home. We would like to meet many of them during future visits back to the place which became so meaningful to us in 1952. It should be interesting to the young people to read about and see how their island really looked almost a half century ago.

Following is a poem given to Bill during our first visit there. This poem eloquently expresses the deep feelings, love and devotion the Caymanians have for their beloved island. The poem would later become Cayman's national song.

Beloved Isle Cayman
by L. E. Ross

O land of soft, fresh breezes, and verdant trees so fair,
With the Creator's glory reflected everywhere.
O sea of palest em'rald, merging to darkest blue,
Whene'er my thoughts fly Godward, I always think of you.

Dear verdant Island, set in blue Caribbean Sea,
I'm coming, coming very soon, O beauteous Isle to thee.
Altho' I've wandered far, my heart enshrines thee yet,
Homeland, fair Cayman Isle, I cannot thee forget.

Away from noise of cities, their fret and carking care,
With moonbeams soft caresses unchecked by garish glare.
Thy fruit with rarest juices, abundant, rich and free,
When sweet church bells are chiming, my fond heart yearns for thee.

When tired of all excitement and glamorous worldly care,
How sweet thy shore to reach, and find a welcome there.
And when comes on the season of "peace, goodwill to men,"
'Tis then I love thee best of all, beloved Isle Cayman.

Lindsay Terry

Rowlett, Texas

Introduction

When Lindsay Terry and Bill Compton visited Grand Cayman in 1952, life in the Cayman Islands was quite different to what it is today. In 1952, we led a tranquil and unhurried lifestyle, with no crime and few visitors. Communication was poor — no telephone service, limited electricity — air conditioning was unheard of! There were few cars and the roads were narrow and unpaved. The West Bay Beach was virtually untouched, and the mosquitoes were ever present! The colour photographs in this book accurately portray what Grand Cayman was like in the early 1950s. In those days few Caymanians took photographs, and colour photographs were even more rare, so we are very fortunate that Lindsay was an amateur photographer!

As a young boy growing up in the islands, I enjoyed the simple pleasures mentioned in this book — swimming, sailing and fishing. Our social life revolved around the Church and family activities. However, life was not all play; parents depended on their children to help with the daily chores.

Due to insufficient job opportunities at home, most Caymanian men were forced to leave the islands. This separation from Cayman was difficult — leaving loved ones behind was not easy, but there was no alternative. Some men found employment in various ports, mostly in the United States, but the majority chose the sea as a career. Many advanced as far as Captain or Chief Engineer on commercial vessels. At one time, there were so many Captains with the same surname, people started calling them by their first names to avoid confusion. For example, Capt. Ebanks could have meant a number of people! This tradition is still observed today.

A turning point in our island's social and economic life was the building of the airstrip which made Grand Cayman more accessible. As the economy improved, more job opportunities arose and the men were able to return home to make their living. The Cayman Islands have progressed far beyond what anyone envisioned, and today we enjoy what is probably the highest standard of living in the Caribbean.

Charles Kirkkconnell, as he appeared in a photo made in the early 1950s.

However, development has not been without cost. We have become more materialistic and drifted away from many of the values earlier Caymanians held dear. This book takes us back in time to when priorities were different. It offers us an opportunity to reflect on what was important to the people of our islands almost half a century ago, family, church, friends, country, respect for parents, older people and those in authority.

This book has been presented in a very informative and interesting manner. It should be of great interest to Caymanians too young to know the unhurried lifestyle of past years, when Caymanians were content with very little. They shared whatever they had with each other and welcomed visitors into their homes; visitors were not considered strangers — just friends they had not already met.

Older Caymanians will enjoy going back in time and will no doubt recall a few memories of their own. I am sure that many will also remember these two enthusiastic young men who arrived on Grand Cayman 47 years ago, armed with their Bibles, music, and cameras. They spent the better part of their summer vacation sharing the Gospel and their lives with the people of Grand Cayman.

Thank you, Lindsay and Bill, for sharing your memories with us.

Charles L. Kirkconnell, O.B.E.
George Town, Grand Cayman

•

Captain Charles L. Kirkconnell, a well-known businessman in the Cayman Islands, became an Officer of the Order of the British Empire in 1991. He and his family reside on Grand Cayman, near George Town.

A Brief History of Grand Cayman

The writer of this volume is in no position to provide the people of Grand Cayman with any portion of their history; however, some will no doubt read this book who are not native Caymanians. Therefore, in this chapter we will pass along a few of the facts that we have come upon as we read numerous historical books and magazines. Some information has been verbally given by older citizens of the island. One earlier Caymanian writer said, "We have little more than tradition to guide us as to the industrial, social and political life of early years."

Christopher Columbus first named the islands after his discovery of Cayman Brac and Little Cayman in 1503. He called them Las Tortugas because of the abundance of turtles. His son, Fernando, wrote in the ship's log, "...we were in sight of two very small and low islands, full of tortoises, as was all the sea about, in so much that they looked like little rocks..."

Some time later the name of the islands was changed to the Caymans. History records that Sir Francis Drake visited in 1586 and wrote in his log that no people lived on the islands and that they were inhabited by "great serpents called Caymanas like large lizards, which are edible." The spelling "CAYMAN" came in the early 1800s. Before that time the name was "Caymanas," and it has appeared in old deeds as "Caimanos," "Kiemanos," and in other ways.

In the late 1700s the population was near 1,000; more than 500 of which were slaves. Because the slave ships' route from Africa was near the Caymans, numerous ships foundered on the island's reefs, leaving many of their human cargo to take their places in the population. After slavery was outlawed in England, slave ships were seized and freed slaves were brought to the island.

The Caymans have some very colourful characters in her past, which include the infamous pirates, Blackbeard (Edward Teach), Anne Bonney, and Sir Henry Morgan. For years the islands proved to be a haven for them and dozens of other maritime robbers.

The Cayman Islands have a long history of wrecked ships off her shores; the most famous of which was the "wreck of the ten sail." Legend has it that in 1788 His Majesty's Ship *Convert* and nine other vessels foundered on the eastern reefs of Grand Cayman. One version of the account is that a prince was aboard one of the ships, whom the people of East End rescued along with other members of the crew. None were lost. As a result, the British monarch, George III, declared the Cayman Islands to be free of taxation and wartime conscription.

The shipwrecks were later confirmed by archaeologist Margaret Leshikar-Denton, who led an expedition in locating dozens of cannons, anchors, ship fittings, ceramics and glass articles.

By 1906 the population of the Cayman Islands had reached 5,000, with 1,500 of them at sea in ships. Many of the seamen were away from their families for up to two years. Some left wives, who were pregnant, and did not see their children until they were toddlers. Until 1952, when the first airstrip was built and Owen Roberts Airfield was dedicated, the economy of Grand Cayman was mainly supported by the money sent home by the seafaring husbands and fathers. A limited amount of industry was realized from rope making, the sale of turtle meat, and shipbuilding.

These economic supporters have given way in recent years to tourism and offshore banking. In the last decade or so, more than 500,000 visitors have annually come to Grand Cayman. There are more than 3,000 offshore financial institutions in George Town, capital city of the Cayman Islands.

The people are harmonious and happy descendants of former slaves, mariners, adventurers and traders. They make up an industrious society, which to this day remains free from racial and religious prejudice.

Grand Cayman is approximately 22 miles long and 4 to 7 miles wide. The crime rate is low and education is good. Food grown on the island includes coconuts, mangoes, breadfruit, plantains, and bananas. There are a number of churches, some of which are United Church (formerly Presbyterian), Church of God, Baptist, and Catholic to name a few.

THE PEOPLE OF GRAND CAYMAN:
As I came to know them

Chapter One

"Their Lives"

In this first chapter I would like to share with you the impressions that I received while living among the people of Grand Cayman for more than two months. In many instances I will not be able to recall their names. I truly regret that, but, I will share my memories with you, describing them with several adjectives that seem appropriate as I look back. They were:

Unhurried

After stepping onshore at North Sound, Grand Cayman, in 1952, we found a people who were truly experiencing an unhurried lifestyle. They were enjoying something that millions of people around the world would love to have — times of leisure in a fast-paced world. There was truly no reason for them to get in a hurry. They knew that life was not going to pass them by.

They were industrious people, but without a deadline to meet. I often saw Caymanians going to and from the marketplace who had left themselves plenty of time to do what was necessary to make the day successful.

We saw men loading and unloading merchant ships. They worked steadily, but didn't seem to be pressed by a tight schedule. We saw clerks in stores busily going about the day's work, yet not fretful. We saw fishermen at the dockside, who had made their way in from the sea with a good catch, leisurely cleaning the rewards of the day, getting them ready

for sale. They didn't seem to have any place to be at any particular time. They laughed and exchanged stories as they kept on with their chore.

Police constables and office workers were carefully taking care of the needs of the people, with a confident, pleasant pace, knowing they were appreciated.

We saw carpenters and painters leave their work with a great deal of light still in the day. That gave them time to make their way home to do the evening chores, play with the children and have a pleasant evening with their families.

Other illustrations could be given, but the above examples give some picture of the unhurried lifestyle of the Grand Caymanians as we found them.

Pleasant

We found the people on Grand Cayman extremely pleasant. We stayed on the island for nearly two and one half months, and do not remember hearing a harsh word from anyone. We're sure they had their times of irritation, quarreling and being generally unhappy, but we did not hear it. This was not an outward show because we were visitors. We observed them in their relationship with each other in the shops, in their homes and on the street corners, and I am still amazed at the pleasantness.

It seemed that mothers had trained children in such a manner that there was not need for harshness or screaming. They had learned respect for each other to the point that they were pleasant to each other in their conversations.

Never did we hear anyone berated or belittled, unless it was in jest. How pleasant it was for us to be among people with those admirable characteristics in their daily lives.

Many were the times at night when we would be making our way back to our quarters after a meeting when we would meet families walking along roads and paths in the darkness. As we passed, we could hear them say, "Good night." The greetings were for

everyone, because in the darkness they could not tell who was passing by.

Unassuming

Not only did the Cayman people refrain from being impressed with themselves, we never heard one take another for granted. They never assumed that anyone owed them anything. They seemed to be content to do their own work and be rewarded for their own accomplishments.

There were many poor people, to be sure, but there seemed to be no outward manifestation that others owed them a living. Yet, I'm sure they were grateful when favors came their way. This leads me into the next topic.

Giving and Sharing

We saw outward signs of a sharing attitude. The two of us would have been in a terrible fix if they had not been generous with us. Not only did they share their food and drink with Bill and me, they shared their homes, their churches, their time, and their recreation. We noticed that they also shared with each other. It is often said by the people of Grand Cayman of those early years, "We lived like one big family."

Helpful

As it concerns this characteristic, Bill and I can speak firsthand. We had only been on Grand Cayman a few moments when we met Captain Ertis Ebanks (that was an affectionate nickname that they gave him), who became our first friend. He met us at North Sound as we came ashore by boat and introduced himself and offered his services. He had a "taxi" business of sorts. He had one of the few cars on the island at that time — actually it was a station wagon. He went above and beyond his remuneration providing needed information about George Town and the surrounding area. He seemed to be genuinely interested in helping us.

The people were most friendly and outgoing, and before long we had become acquainted with a great number of the islanders. Nearly all of the men on the island wore mustaches. Since we were so young (Bill was 22 and I was only 19), the men advised us to grow mustaches to make us look a little more mature. So we undertook the project with great resolve. To give our mustaches (which were really only fuzz), a degree of credence, we put a little mustache wax on them, which we obtained from the local barber, who had become our friend.

Then there was the dear housekeeper of the Seaview Hotel, Rosa, a thoughtful lady who helped and encouraged us in so many ways, not the least of which were her offerings of turtle meat sandwiches left on our dresser at night, following our meetings.

There were so many others such as the Ashford Panton family, the McTaggarts, the Merrens, Rev. James Davis, interim pastor of Elmslie Church, and the kind family at North Side, just to name a few.

Diligent

In spite of a lack of modern conveniences and wealth enjoyed by so many others in other parts of the world, Caymanians seemed to have the determination to make their lives count and to take advantage of every opportunity afforded them. They seemed to be content with doing today what could and should be done, trusting that the overall result would be to their benefit and to the benefit of their children.

This diligence was not only observed in the lives of individuals but in the collective efforts of the community.

Respectful to Others

We went to the island, not expecting to be received in any particular manner, because we knew nothing about the people and their island. We received respect from them, not because of who we were but because we were visitors in their homeland. There was evidence that they were not about to bring any

reproach on themselves or their island home.

They had a tremendous degree of respect for those in authority. I never saw a trace of disrespect or heard a word of resentfulness. They had regard for their friends and neighbors. Children held their parents in high esteem, and parents were lovingly respectful to the children.

There are a number of other characteristics that could be described in detail, but I'll only mention two others, their interest in others and their industriousness.

Such were the lives of the people of Grand Cayman — as I observed them.

Chapter Two

"Their Loves"

A number of things seemed very dear to the people of Grand Cayman. I will mention a few of them, in the order of importance that I feel they placed them.

Family

As in other places where I have traveled, I did not find children who were neglected or seemed to be in any way unhappy. Of course, because of their childish nature we're sure they had unhappy times, but there seemed to be a complete sense of devotion to family on the part of the parents and the children.

Home

As in many parts of the world, homes on Grand Cayman ranged from the lowliest shanty to the large and stately. Yet, it seemed that in each one, where a family dwelt, there was a love for home. It was a place where they were always welcomed and could share their love with the rest of the family.

Church

Church attendance, as I observed it, seemed to be very good, which indicated to us that the people loved their churches and their pastors. They seemed to receive a great deal of satisfaction from their faith in God and their assurance that happiness could be found in activities surrounding the church.

All of the people of Grand Cayman did not attend services regularly, but it was my observation that a great many of them had high regard for their church, Christian teachings and their church leaders.

As in the U.S., many of the Cayman people had a knowledge of the Bible but had never personally accepted God's promises. Although some, from their childhood, were completely conversant with Scripture passages such as John 3:16, ("For God so loved the world, that He gave His only begotten Son, that whosoever believeth in Him should not perish, but have everlasting life."), they had never personally embraced it. We invited them to do just that and many of them did so.

On a recent trip back to Grand Cayman I met several people who confirmed that they had made those decisions in 1952, and I am happy to report that they have remained faithful to their commitment for nearly half a century.

Friends

On occasions we had opportunity to observe friends working together or just strolling down the street together, engaged in conversation. There seemed to be a sincerity about them and their relationship to each other.

Their Island

The people of Grand Cayman truly loved their island. We found a sincere, deep and abiding respect for their homeland. Their love and appreciation was evidenced in their daily conversation, their poetry and their letters to those off the island. They took pride in showing us points of interest.

It would have been hard to live among the citizens of Grand Cayman and not observe their affection for their island home. They possessed a degree of balance that helped them to keep all of these things in the right perspective. Of course, in my opinion, not everyone had his head "screwed on" right, but the population in general seemed to have a healthy perspective toward their island home.

In a folder containing memorabilia from our 1952 trip is a card sent to Bill by Innis Bodden. It was a picture postcard of Church Street, looking north and showing among other things, the Elmslie Memorial Church. It bears a caption, *"Greetings from Grand Cayman, BWI,"* with a poem which reflects their love for the island.

Greetings from the land of Sunshine,
Down where the skies are blue,
Where many charms await you,
In a perfect rendezvous.

Basking on a beach unrivaled,
While the trade winds whisper low:
"Welcome to the Land of Sunshine
From the northern sleet and snow."

Here in dreamy Cayman Island
You'll find nature at play,
And you'll drive away your troubles
With a perfect holiday.

Chapter Three

"Their Living"

Keep it in mind as you read this account that there was a broad range of financial standing among the people. It is not my purpose to draw undue attention to that fact. Those conditions exist all over the world and have existed since early history. I am not in a position to explain why some seemed quite wealthy while others were very poor. It was, however, a fact of life on Grand Cayman in the early 1950s. Characteristics of their living were:

Wealthy

A few of the people lived quite sumptuously. They would have been considered wealthy by today's standards in any society. Some had been educated off the island and had gone back to give their families and friends the benefit of their schooling and training. They owned businesses, lands and other possessions, lived in large beautiful homes and, comparatively speaking, were the affluent of Grand Cayman.

Bill and I found some of those people to be among our most ardent supporters. They assisted us in any way that seemed possible to them or us. For that we remain grateful. That gave us some contact with people in high places.

Let us hasten to say that the affluent seemed to realize that they were governed by the same laws and regulations as the balance of the population. There did not seem to be any resentment of the more wealthy by those of less means. There was a genuine appreciation for them, because the majority of the people realized that the wealth of the few brought a better life to everyone. For instance, ships owned by the Webster family and Mr. H. O. Merren, who also owned a dry goods store, brought goods and supplies to the island on a regular basis. Mr. Ashford Panton was the proprietor of a hardware store and a small restaurant. Mr. Ernest Panton and Mr. Albert Panton were qualified, when needed, to step into the position of Acting Commissioner, until a permanent Commissioner could be appointed. Dr. McTaggart, the island's only dentist, also owned a general merchandise store as well as the Seaview Hotel, a small establishment with about four guest rooms available. It remains to this day, as a larger hotel.

There seemed to be a true friendship between many of the rich and the poor.

Poor

Poorer and less educated people did not seem to be in despair because they realized that there were many intangible, valuable things they possessed, which they could not purchase with money. Among these were family, friends, and the ability to react to tough circumstances. There did not seem to be many families who were completely destitute.

We did see, in different places on the island, houses in various stages of completion. Some were grown up in weeds because they had not been worked on in more than a year, sometimes two or three. The owners worked on them as they were able, as the money could be earned and made available. Some of the men had to go to sea for as much as a year, sometimes more. Many of these small houses took years to build. While building them, they lived in homes with no electricity or inside bathrooms. In most of the smaller homes there were not places to cook inside the house. They had what they called a cookroom behind the house. Cooking was done on a small open hearth or fireplace. Baking was done in a homemade oven.

Through it all the people of much lesser means were not resentful. They took life as it was dealt to them and made the best of it, living each day to the fullest.

Middle Income

As might be expected, most of the people fell into the middle income category. They were people with jobs and positions in the towns around the island. These places of employment and labour will be explained in a later chapter. The middle income families were truly a stabilizing force. Many of them were leaders in their communities and in their churches. They dressed well when the occasion demanded it and took pride in their accomplishments. Hundreds, thousands by now, have gone away from those families to schools of higher learning.

Frugal

One thing that can be said of the Caymanian people is that they did not spend money unwisely. Most of them tried to save a good portion of all they made. They, of course, did not have large shopping malls and department stores. They were not pressed to buy the latest model cars or the most recent appliances. They were content to live simple lives and put back as much as possible for the future, for themselves and for their children.

No Racial Barriers

We went to Grand Cayman, as has been stated, as young men from the Southern part of the United States. Our home town was Decatur, Alabama, the heart of the deep South. At that time our part of the country was steeped in racial discord. We had no idea what we would find in Grand Cayman. We found a place where these topics were not discussed nor thought about to a great extent. There was absolutely no emphasis placed on integration or segregation of the races, yet we found, in certain situations, a definite form of segregation.

To my surprise, when I attended my first service at Elmslie Church, I saw people of colour sitting on one side of the church and the white people on the other. There seemed to be a sprinkling of coloured people on the white side and a few white people on the coloured side. It seemed to be something that they observed subconsciously, as though it were a part of their history.

On at least one occasion I heard music at night, in the distance. Upon inquiring about what was going on, I was told that the coloured people were having a dance. Again, I thought that very unusual, so I asked, "Why just the coloured people?" The answer was, "That's just the way it is usually done." Perhaps one reason that I found it hard to understand was that I saw absolutely no evidence of segregation in the schools, in the work place, in the shops or on the streets where people usually met to chat. I saw numbers of mixed race couples, and I saw many children who were the offspring of racially mixed parents. In all of this the people lived in harmony and respect for each other.

Progressive

One of the great passions of the people was their desire to see their children educated. Great emphasis was placed on the training and developing of their offspring. Often parents sent their children to other countries after high school to receive further education.

They were industrious to the point that a turtle soup factory was built on the island, which employed a number of people. Poorer families spent many hours making rope to be sold and exported. Agriculture was limited, but they did as much as possible, raising plantains, breadfruit, mangoes, bananas and some pineapples.

Small hotels were started to encourage visitors and a limited amount of tourism. These hotels employed a few people, besides the carpenters, painters, electricians, and other workers who helped build them.

Chapter Four

"Their Labour"

Cayman people seemed to enjoy progress because hard work didn't seem to discourage or deter them. If there were jobs to do, they did them. To be sure, as you will see in at least one of the pictures in this book, there were times when you could find dozens of people gathered in groups, laughing and talking as they shared the happenings of the day. Usually, if you found people gathered with seemingly nothing to do, it was in the late afternoon or in the evening, after their daily tasks were completed. We had no way of knowing exactly who was gainfully employed. Following are some of the areas of their labour that we observed:

In Stores and Shops

Since there were plenty of stores that seemed to be well-stocked, there naturally had to be an adequate number of clerks to run them. The clerks were very helpful and served with enthusiasm and friendliness. Bill and I often dropped in to make small purchases and at the same time were able to gather information about the island.

Agriculture and Live Stock

Most of the agriculture was done on a very small scale by individuals who sold portions of their crop to help their financial situation. Some of them sold bananas, plantains, mangoes, breadfruit or other fresh foods. They sold them on the streets or delivered them to the homes.

A few of the residents had cows and chickens. They often sold eggs and milk to neighbors. There was a limited amount of beef, chicken and fish eaten.

Civil Service

There was a small number of people who worked in public offices such as the customs department, the government building, the constables' offices, the courts, and the post office, to name a few.

Schools

Grand Cayman had an effective school system for the island children and teens. They had a well-trained faculty who prepared the young people for life as adults, whether they planned to go on to higher education in other countries or remain on the island. They gave an extensive exam during the last year of high school to see if the students could receive their diplomas or would have to repeat their last year, during which they would take the test again.

Small Hotels

As has already been described, there were two small hotels which employed a limited number of people.

Turtle Soup Factory

Near North Sound was a turtle soup factory which employed a few people and sold turtle soup to other markets, including all of the Cayman Islands. The turtle pens which kept the large turtles brought from the Florida Keys were in North Sound. The pens can be seen in a few of the pictures in this volume.

Fishing

Some of the men of the island would go out to sea a short distance where they often made excellent catches of fish which they would sell to the residents when they returned to the docks. One picture in this book shows two men selling their catch.

Going to Sea

Almost since the islands were inhabited, most of the Caymanian men made their living as seamen. During our stay on Grand Cayman, it was true that much of the economy of the island was supported by the money sent home by these seafaring men. It was a hard life, but the only life that many of the men knew.

Rope Making

Many of the families of the Cayman Islands spent most of their spare time making rope. It was manufactured from the thatch palm leaves grown in abundance near their homes. The rope was strong and durable and was sought out by sailing vessels and other rope users. It was used mainly by turtle fishermen and was exported to Jamaica. It reportedly was easy to handle and very durable in salt water so Jamaican fishermen used it to set their traps in deep water.

On the Docks

When the *Caymania* and the *Merco* were in dock, there were a few jobs available loading and unloading cargo and making repairs to the large boats.

Miscellaneous Jobs

A number of men were very talented as craftsmen such as painters, carpenters, stone masons, etc. There was a limited amount of employment for these men, since little building was going on during these times.

Some women were used as domestics in the larger homes. Young men were employed as yard boys or to do other odd jobs around the homes where they were employed.

The above descriptions give a limited view of employment as we found it in 1952. It is, admittedly, incomplete, but perhaps gives some idea of how some of the people made a living for their families.

Chapter Five

"Their Leisure"

Although Grand Cayman is now one of the world's most popular resort centers, with recreational and rest opportunities on every side and with hundreds of cruise ships stopping each year, it was not always so. Yet, the people of the island found times for rest and relaxation in 1952 that took other forms, for the most part, than those enjoyed today.

Beaches

There were always the beautiful beaches, yet they were practically unused by most of the island people. Bill and I were unable to understand that. Only very occasionally would we see someone enjoying the beaches. We often saw young boys and teenagers swimming in the clear waters around Hog Sty Bay, but not on the beaches.

Tennis

A few of the people, mostly teens, had access to Dr. Roy McTaggart's tennis court along side his house. That was the only tennis court that we saw on the island.

Napping

One leisurely activity that the ladies tried to enjoy in the afternoons, when most of the chores were done, was a restful nap in the hammock. As we stated in another place, many of the homes had hammocks in the bedrooms, stretched from one corner of the room to the opposite one. Although the bed was available, they preferred the hammock for a nap because it was much cooler.

Chatting

In the evenings, people would come out of their homes and congregate along the sea wall to chat, sharing the events of the day. Often, in the cool of the day, we would see people sitting outside their homes, catching a few moments of relaxation. Many times neighbors would stop by for a chat.

Church Socials

On occasions churches would furnish social activities for their people. Activities included beach picnics, concerts (plays) - music as well as drama, garden parties and bazaars. Each church had an annual bazaar which often enjoyed island-wide attendance. Although bicycles were used for transportation, many participated in bike riding as a pastime.

Sailing

On the north side of the island young boys became very adept at sailing small sailboats. Their skill was almost unbelievable. The sea seems to be a bit more rough on the north side of the island, making their feats all the more unusual.

Night Spots

There were a very few night spots that attracted visitors, as well as island people, to drink and dance. They were not well-attended, but did offer some leisure activity for certain ones who chose to participate.

Dances

Occasionally dances would be held at the town halls — each community seemed to have some sort of meeting place, apart from the churches. The dances were not well attended, due in part to the religious convictions of some of the churches.

Sporting Events

There were some sporting events, such as boxing and sailing. We saw one of the boxing matches which featured two of the notable boxers on the island. That sport was very popular among the men. They had access to magazines and some news about boxing in the United States. Joe Louis, a world champion boxer at that time, was a hero to many of the Cayman men.

It is reported that there were cat boat races every Easter, but we did not have an opportunity to enjoy those events.

Travel

A great deal of pleasure travel was not an option for most of the people, yet some were financially able to make trips to other countries. Many of them did, however, make trips to the sister islands of Cayman Brac and Little Cayman. Caymanian seamen traveled extensively, often taking the *Merco* to Tampa, Florida, in order to join other ships.

The Arrival of the Ships and the Plane

When the *Caymania,* the *Merco,* and the seaplane arrived, there were usually small crowds to witness it. Some wanted to see who was arriving on their island while others simply wanted to witness the weekly and monthly events. It was an opportunity to see other people and to chat with them.

Crafts

Some islanders were very artistic and displayed their skills with crafts that they made for themselves and others. The artifacts were usually Cayman Island related. For instance, some were very skillful at taking smaller turtle shells — 18 inches long or a little less — smoothing the backs and making them look glossy. Trinkets were made from shells of varying kinds and sizes. Other crafts sold in 1952 included place mats, baskets and handbags.

THE PLACE CALLED GRAND CAYMAN: As I came to know her

Chapter Six

"The Landscape"

The makeup of Grand Cayman serves as an advantage, since there are so many aspects of the island that make it a desirable place to visit. That is confirmed in the fact that more than 500,000 visitors find their way there each year. In the opinion of this writer, she was much more beautiful in 1952, because we could experience the island in a much more natural, undisturbed state than today. Let me take you back in time to that pristine island home of 7,500 people. Consider the following characteristics:

Size

In 1952, by using a bicycle or other of the limited means of transportation, we could traverse the whole of the island in a short span of time. This allowed us to visit and enjoy all of the island without a great deal of effort.

Green

Because of the generous amount of rainfall we found the island to be a paradise of green foliage, with flowers of many descriptions growing everywhere. The green, vibrant foliage greatly contributed to the freshness in the air.

Beaches

Our most vivid memory of Grand Cayman, as we look back, was the beautiful beach, at that time called West Bay Beach. We were so fascinated that we could ride our bicycles out the lane toward the beach and would only see a small house or

two along the way, usually on the east side of the road away from the beach. I remember thinking as we strolled along the beach, "I can't believe that the people of Grand Cayman don't spend more time out here." We seldom saw anyone on the beach. The thing that was so shocking was that we had known of the famous beaches around the world, and we could not imagine that they were more beautiful than the place where we were standing.

There were numerous small beaches all around the island. Our favorite smaller beach was what is now called Smith Cove. I'm not sure it had a name at that time. We would go out in the early morning hours for daily Scripture reading and prayer. It was such a wonderful place in which to be shut away from the world. After our Scripture reading and prayer, we would go for a swim, diving off the rocks and swimming back in to the beach area — very carefully minding the barracuda.

Historic Places

There were a few places on the island that let us know of activities in earlier centuries. Two such places were the ruins of the old fort in George Town and Pedro's Castle. Although Pedro's Castle is a very popular tourist attraction today, in 1952 it was in disrepair, so tourists were not usually taken to see it. There were numerous places along the seaside where ships and yachts had been built for many years.

Standing as a sentry in George Town, in the front of the Town Hall, was the Clock Tower, erected in the early 1900s to honor King George V of England. It remains to this day, just as it was built.

View of the Sea

As with the other Cayman Islands, Cayman Brac and Little Cayman, most of the homes and businesses were near the sea, taking advantage of the beautiful view of the crystal clear water. The sea had so many shades of colour, according to the depth of the water and the amount

of coral underneath.

George Town, a seacoast village, had the most beautiful view of the sea that one could imagine. The businesses, homes and churches were built in such a position as to take advantage of this unique scenery.

Villages

The largest of the villages on Grand Cayman was George Town, with its tiny shops, small hotels, stores and government buildings. Several thousand people lived there. Surrounding the island were many other smaller villages such as West Bay, North Side, Bodden Town, East End, and Old Man Bay, just to name a few. It was intriguing to go from village to village, talking to the people and being welcomed by them.

Schooners Arriving on the Horizon

A sight that we had often envisioned and had only seen in movies and in books was experienced a few weeks after our arrival. Suddenly one evening about dusk, there appeared on the horizon the silhouette of a schooner, bringing a load of mahogany wood and other merchandise. Also on the ship were seamen, Caymanians who hadn't been home for many long months. There was joy on the island that night. That sight was observed several times during our stay.

Homes

Many of the homes found on the island today were standing in 1952. One has only to look around and inquire of the older people as to their locations. The homes varied in size and worth from the most humble shanty to the large, two-story dwellings. Some of each kind can now be found. Near George Town the home of the Ashford Panton family, a two-story house with porches around the first and second levels, has been restored. The "Pink House" still standing in West Bay was a typical middle-class home in 1952.

Buildings

The most famous and oldest of the buildings on Grand Cayman, is the structure that houses the Cayman Islands Museum, formerly the Old Courts Building. Other buildings and sites of interest were Elmslie Memorial Church and War Memorial, the Post Office, Library, Town Hall and the Clock Tower. They have all been named Historic Sites by the National Trust. Webster's Warehouse was also a prominent structure in 1952. Certainly I want to mention the beautiful homes such as those built by the Pantons, the Merrens, and the McTaggarts, to name a few.

Street Scenes

One of the signs of a carefree society in Grand Cayman was the relaxed street scenes. People could often be seen strolling along the village roads, stopping to chat with friends and acquaintances. Late in the afternoons, when work chores were done, people would gather along the seawall in George Town or sit in front of the stores, sharing news of the day.

There seemed to be very little clutter or trash to make the streets unsightly. People took pride in their communities. In the neighborhoods the homes looked well-cared for with the yards kept very neat.

We never observed any hustle and bustle or hurrying to and fro. People always seemed to have plenty of time to get to their destination or to do the things which needed their attention.

Ships in Harbour

The only things that gave any appearance of a bustling harbour town was when the *Caymania* or the *Merco* were in the harbour, loading or unloading their passengers and merchandise.

The Plane Landing

The most exciting times of the week were when the seaplane would come from Tampa. Small groups of people would go out from George Town to see the landing on North Sound. It truly was a spectacle to see the large PBY sit down on the water, which always seems to be smooth because of the reefs which lock the rough water out of the Sound.

Places of Interest

The place which had been named "Hell" was a spectacle of sorts. The sharp, dark gray, iron-like rock that protruded upward was similar in shape to flames. There were several acres of this formation which attracted visitors.

Today it is much more of an attraction. A postal station has been established there so that tourist can have mail postmarked from "HELL."

As has been mentioned, West Bay Beach (now Seven Mile Beach) and smaller beaches, such as Smith Cove, a short distance from George Town in the other direction, were very interesting places.

Chapter Seven

"The Latitude"

The climate of the Cayman Islands, for that time of the year — July and August — was excellent. We had been accustomed to very hot summers with temperatures of 100 degrees Fahrenheit or better. The island, lying in the latitude of the trade winds, was blessed with cooling breezes, even on the warmest days. We never saw the temperature more than 84 degrees. Only when the winds would veer to the southeast would one feel some oppression.

During a cooler spell the temperature could drop into the 70s, especially in late evening or early morning. We had heavy showers at times, making the mosquito problem worse, although we did have a short respite from the mosquitoes for the first 2 or 3 days after a heavy rain. We were told that the rain would beat them down. The average yearly rainfall on Grand Cayman was about 60 inches.

The weather was always very pleasant for outside activities most any time of the day. Because of the pleasantness of the climate, we had no difficulties with bicycle riding, walking, playing tennis, or other outdoor activities.

I was fair complexioned and had to keep myself protected from the sun. I learned that early on. I went for a stroll behind the Seaview Hotel the first day we moved into that establishment. I was without a shirt and was so badly sunburned in about 45 minutes that I had to use remedies to make sure that it did not get out of hand.

We were told that the most pleasant season on Grand Cayman was from November to April. During those months there were very few mosquitoes. We understood also that the hurricane season was generally from June to November. We never experienced anything of that sort, although one hurricane came close to the island during the latter part of our stay. I am grateful the island was spared on that occasion.

Chapter Eight

"The Liabilities"

It is difficult to imagine the Grand Cayman that I saw in 1952 as a place with liabilities. I'm sure that those who were born there and those visitors who came to love her, found Grand Cayman, in the early days, a near perfect place to live. However, we will list what might be considered liabilities by today's standards in other parts of the world. Consider the following:

Mosquitoes

I have described this problem in other parts of this volume, so it is enough for me to state that the mosquitoes made the island's night-time activities most uncomfortable.

The "flit gun" (a hand pumped apparatus with a fluid container on the front) was the most effective means of mosquito control inside the home. Spraying a mist around the room and onto the screens, if the house had screens, would control the pests enough to make the home livable.

Bill Compton declares that he was awakened one night by a conversation between two mosquitoes. One was saying to the other, "We had better take these guys and hide them before the bigger ones come and take them away from us."

A Lack of Transportation

Only by today's standards could one say that a lack of transportation was a liability in 1952. However, it was true that the only methods of going to or leaving Grand Cayman were the air boats (the converted Navy PBYs), which came once each week, and the small ships, the *Caymania* and the *Merco*, which came approximately twice each month. They all came from and returned to Tampa, Florida. The limited number of cars on the island were brought there by boat. Public transportation was limited to the trucks with seats mounted on the beds and one "taxi," operated by

Ertis Ebanks, later known as Captain Ertis.

Many of the people rode bicycles. Most walked to places where they wanted to go. Those who were privileged to have automobiles were generous to the extent that they often offered rides to those walking

A Lack of Conveniences

Even with a lack of "modern" conveniences, the Cayman people had carved out happy lives for themselves. Their ability to adapt to the "hand" they were dealt was remarkable. They improvised and invented methods to improve their existence. They accepted the limitations of their conveniences with a resolve that even led their children to become happy contributors to better family living.

Electricity was furnished only a few hours each day. Consequently, no refrigeration was available to the general public. Some of the more affluent could afford generators and fuel to run their electrical appliances. As I remember, the public electric supply was from five o'clock in the afternoon until ten o'clock at night.

Fresh water was limited to the supply from wells and cisterns. Cisterns were large receptacles that were filled as rain water was caught from the roofs of houses by a system of gutters and metal or wooden channels.

Some of the poorer families had to carry each day's water supply from a central location, usually a public place where they could fill their containers. Teens and young children in the families were very helpful with these tasks.

Washing the family's clothes was a task performed mostly out of doors, using small tubs, scrub boards and boiling pots. The ironing was done with an iron that had to be heated on the stove in the kitchen or over a charcoal fire. Some of the irons were "flat irons" with only a handle, while others had a steam mechanism attached to them.

News of the outside world was learned from shortwave radios, magazines and papers brought by the seaplane, the *Caymania* and the

Merco. Mail was sent and received in much the same way.

Hurricanes

Some of the more modern buildings that were enjoyed in 1952 were buildings that had been rebuilt following the devastating hurricane of 1932. Cayman Brac and Little Cayman were hit with unbelievable tragedy and loss of lives. While Bill and I were on Grand Cayman, a hurricane went through the area, missing the islands.

During that time a barge was on the way to the island bringing equipment to build an airstrip. It was behind schedule and communication with it was lost. It was feared that the hurricane had sunk it. As it turned out, the heavy metal equipment on board caused the compass to be affected and finding the island was difficult for the crew on board.

In recent years the hurricanes have caused some damage, but no lives have been lost.

Little Usable Land Area

Because of a lack of suitable farming acreage, only a few crops could be raised. A greater portion of the island was covered with swamp vegetation, except in the eastern portion which had an abundance of wooded area. Much of the food used by the people of Grand Cayman had to be shipped to the island. However, they did enjoy what seemed a plenteous supply of certain foods such as plantains, breadfruit, mangoes, pineapples, bananas, seagrapes, yams, and almonds, to name a few. There was enough land for a few head of cattle from which they could have a limited supply of milk and beef.

Most of the farm acreage was cleared and prepared with great effort and with very little equipment. The land on which the houses were built was very inexpensive, even at 1952 prices. The beach proper, which is today Seven Mile Beach, could be purchased for less than $20.00 per front foot. As of this writing it sells for $35,000 to $40,000 per front foot or more than 2,000 times the 1952 price.

"The Long Look Into the Future"

Some of the Grand Cayman residents had a tremendous vision for the future. We left the island the day after the barges landed bringing the earth-moving equipment to build the first airstrip. It was easy to see what the future could hold, with the financial situation and the beautiful seven miles of beach, yet we're sure no one could have envisioned what is happening today.

Transportation

Even though we were inexperienced young men, we could see what the airstrip would do for the economy and for the advancement of the living conditions on the island. Better transportation would bring more tourists, which would use bigger and better hotels, restaurants, support shops, and businesses. It would also mean more convenient travel for Caymanians, in times of real medical needs and business opportunities. It would mean more and better jobs for Caymanians.

Beaches

The beaches, especially West Bay Beach, would bring visitors by the hundreds of thousands — simply because it is one of the most beautiful in the world. Magnificent resort hotels and other establishments would be built. The first major hotel was built in 1973, some 21 years after our visit. The beautiful, clear water and the reefs surrounding the island would bring divers from around the world. Land costs would skyrocket!

Taxes

The tax situation would attract businesses from every corner of the globe. This also would bring new jobs for the people of the island. With the airstrip and the businesses would come resorts, paved roads, and modern living conditions. Travel to and from the island would be done in hours instead of weeks and months.

Notable Changes

With the coming of a half million visitors each year — by cruise ships and jet airplanes — would come wholesale changes to support tourism of that magnitude. The untouched, pristine beauty, which had lasted for centuries, would give way to hotels, tall buildings, hundreds of gift shops, automobiles and diving locations. With these changes would come limitless opportunities for the Cayman people — jobs, investment opportunities, better educational institutions, and hospitals. Large shopping markets would make available most all of the needs of the good life.

Grand Cayman would become one of the most popular vacation spots in the Caribbean and a very pleasant place for the Cayman people to live.

The photographs you will find on the following pages are a pictorial account of much of our 1952 visit to Grand Cayman. Words fail me when I try to express how much I hope the Cayman people, especially those living in Grand Cayman during our first visit, will enjoy seeing them. I have added a feature to this book that I hope you will find interesting. I call it...

THEN...   ...and NOW.

During a 1994 visit to Grand Cayman, I went to some of the same places that I photographed in 1952 and photographed what is there now.
You will see the results as you continue looking through the book.

The thatched-covered waiting shelter at North Sound was adjacent to the Customs Building. Although the temperature never rose above the mid-80s, it provided protection from the direct sun for small groups who were waiting for the seaplane to arrive or to board it for departure.

Previous pages:

THEN...

A scene at Cardinal Avenue and Harbour Drive. The small building on the right was a gasoline station operated by Sunbeam Thompson. In the centre was a notice board. On the left were Will Coe's shop and Willie Bodden's barber shop.

...and NOW

A very busy, modern street corner, and as before, right on the harbour. A lot of activity goes on at this location. Tourists from the cruise ships are brought to the small shelter in the centre of the picture.

The *Merco* being unloaded at the harbour in George Town. It had recently come from Tampa, Florida, with passengers, lumber and other merchandise. It was always a welcomed sight.

Fishermen back with the day's catch, selling the fish to people waiting on the dock. The fish were cleaned and dressed right there in the boat. Children gathered to watch the process. This scene is on the waterfront in George Town Harbour. Fish was a valuable commodity for the people and quite inexpensive.

Bill Compton, standing on the pier that extended from the Customs Building at North Sound, filming the slaughter of giant turtles. Bill was using a small 8mm movie camera, with which he captured many aspects of our visit. The original film is now owned by the Cayman Islands National Archive, Dr. Philip Pedley, Director. The turtle meat was sold in an open market to the Cayman people. Large portions of the meat were taken to the turtle soup factory nearby.

The Ashford Panton family and friends walking out to
the end of the pier at North Sound, accompanying Mark
Panton, who was leaving for college on the seaplane.
People in the photograph are (from left) Theda Panton
(now Schreckengraft), Mrs. Ashford (Phyllis) Panton,
Mark, Winsome Panton Yanes and a friend, Keith
Thompson. The young boy is Winsome's son, Joey.

A seaplane taking off from North Sound. The relatively calm water was protected from the open sea by the reefs. This photo reveals the beautiful blue waters in North Sound, always enjoyed by the Cayman people.

Young boys were often used to care for odd jobs. They were too young to go to sea; therefore, these opportunities for employment were welcomed. Their wheelbarrow is loaded with used batteries.

The building in the background (centre) is the customs warehouse. The building to the left of it is Dr. Malley McTaggart's shop. To the right of it is the gasoline station.

The seaplane, a converted Navy PBY amphibian, making its approach to North Sound. It is the same plane that brought Bill Compton and me to Grand Cayman from Tampa, Florida. This plane could land on the water in North Sound and on a runway in Tampa.

Previous pages:

THEN...

This corner, Harbour Drive at Shedden Road, was the busiest part of Grand Cayman. To the right is the seawall and George Town Harbour. The white building on the left was Webster's store or warehouse. The yellow building next to it was the old Presbyterian manse. The white building on the side toward the sea was Malley Coe's shop.

...and NOW

This scene has been modernized, yet some of the buildings remain the same. Pavement, traffic signals and automobiles have been added. This is one of the first scenes the tourist from the cruise ships see on Grand Cayman.

A very interesting bird, a Man-Of-War, picks up a morsel from the bay in George Town. The fishermen (out of the picture to the left) have thrown scraps from their fish cleaning into the water. The birds made a feast of them.

The *Merco* is in port. This scene is just in front of the seawall near the Old Courts Building, now the Cayman Islands Museum.

Fishermen just off shore in Hog
Sty Bay near George Town.
Fishing at this short distance from
the shore was often quite good.

A young child enjoying the day in George Town. After daily chores, life was filled with "things to do" for children. Much of their fun and recreation was born out of their own imagination. Fishermen are in the boat just off shore. In the upper right background, a few of the buildings of George Town can be seen.

Rope, handmade by Caymanian families, being off-loaded from the truck at the dock in George Town. It will later be loaded onto either the *Caymania* or the *Merco* and shipped to other islands and nations. Many families spent hours each day making this kind of rope. It was made from leaves taken from thatch palm trees near their homes and was considered very strong and durable. Many of the Jamaican fishermen used it to lower their traps into very deep water. It was unusually strong in salt water.

A beautiful Cayman house, much like many other homes scattered about the island. Some are still standing and are being used to this day.

A rear view of the Seaview Hotel on South Church Street, where Bill and I stayed. It had been open for about one year and had approximately four rooms for rent. It was, at this time, being expanded. It later became much larger and is a busy hotel to this day.

A late afternoon gathering in downtown George Town near the seawall. The building in the foreground was Ethel Cook-Bodden's Yankee Notion Shoppe. Bill Compton is the person in the white shirt on the bicycle in the rear of the group.

Constables stand at attention on the pier at North
Sound as Andrew M. Gerrard, the new Commissioner,
passes. He is flanked by Major Roddy Whatler (left) and
Acting Commissioner Albert "Bertie" Panton. Gerrard
has just arrived on the seaplane. The Customs Building
is in the background.

The pier that leads from the
Customs Building to a sheltered
area where passengers from the
seaplane were brought. Turtle
pens at right are visible.

Turtle pens in the shallow water near the shore of North Sound. Turtle fishermen would bring the mammoth creatures, sometimes five or six hundred pounds in weight, from other locations beyond the Caribbean. They were kept here until time to slaughter them for the turtle meat factory. They were often killed and dressed and the meat sold in open markets in nearby towns. It was necessary to quickly sell the freshly prepared meat since refrigeration was very limited.

This unusual rock-like formation that resembled flames was called "Hell" by the locals. The young, deaf lad had feet tough enough to allow him to walk barefoot on the sharp, jagged peaks. In those early years this was a place where visitors were sometimes taken. Today it is a very popular tourist attraction.

THEN...

A Sunday school class in front of Elmslie Memorial Church. Some of the people shown in this photograph may recognize themselves as they see the above picture. Numbers of them still live on Grand Cayman. Church services and activities were very important to the Cayman people.

Previous pages:

Quiet, picturesque Fort Street, looking toward the waterfront. The yellow building was Dobson Hall, given by Col. Dobson for the Scouts in the 1930s. It was used as a Home Guard barracks in WWII. The fort and famous cotton tree, used as a lookout point during the war, is just beyond it. The building in the foreground was Ashford Panton's store. The white fence on the left was in front of Captain Ben Grainger's house. To the left of the pedestrian was Eddie Parson's house.

...and NOW

Elmslie Memorial Church as it appears today. This George Town landmark, built in 1920, and approximately 90 other churches on the island, are very important to the Cayman people, with Sunday services well attended. Christianity is the predominant religion of the Cayman Islands whose Coat of Arms bears an inscription from Psalms 24:2, "He hath founded it upon the seas." There is very little commercial activity on Sundays, except for restaurants. Sunday in the Cayman Islands is considered a day of rest.

THEN...

Looking toward Edward Street
from the Town Hall area. Guides
and Guards are in formation to
welcome the new Commissioner,
Andrew Gerrard. The people of
Grand Cayman went to great
lengths to make this a meaningful
occasion.

...and NOW

Scenes like this made me feel I was in a different place when I returned for the first time in 1994. The old ways had given way to new methods. The dirt roads of 1952 had now become beautiful paved streets. Magnificent buildings had been constructed, making George Town a modern city. An older building, the Public Library, seen on the extreme left, was there in 1952.

The man on the left, who was
deaf, was keeper of the turtle
pens in West Bay. On his left is Bill
Compton along with Ertis Ebanks.

Turtles were kept in these pens. You can see behind the
keeper the fences that protrude down through the water and
into the ground. Smaller turtles were kept here. Large ones,
that ranged up to 500 pounds and more, were kept in the
pens at North Sound.

A schooner anchored in Hog Sty
Bay near George Town. These
smaller, sail-driven ships for many
years brought needed
merchandise to the island. Many
of the Cayman men sailed in these
ships.

A sharply dressed constable is standing on the pier awaiting the arrival of the seaplane bringing Andrew Gerrard, the new Commissioner. The Customs Building is in the background.

A scene on Edward Street. Guides and Guards are in formation to welcome Commissioner Gerrard. Many Cayman citizens have come out to witness this occasion. To the left is the Public Library building, which is still in use today.

Acting Commissioner Albert Panton (left), and Major
Roddy Whatler (right), usher Andrew Gerrard, the new
Commissioner, to the Town Hall for his installation.
Guides and Guards are in the background. The Public
Library building is on the left. This scene is on Edward
Street.

THEN...

Ertis Ebanks (left) led Bill Compton into
"Hell." There are several acres of this strange
phenomenon. The rock formations resemble
flames. Only their sturdy-soled shoes
allowed them to stand on the stone spikes.

...and NOW

Marilyn Terry (left) and a tourist stand on a platform built to allow people to see "Hell" without being tempted to wander dangerously into it. This platform is directly behind a small post office and a gift shop. Visitors can have post cards and letters postmarked from "HELL."

Previous pages:

THEN...

On the right is the Old Courts Building, one of the oldest buildings in Cayman, now the home of the Cayman Islands Museum. Out front, facing Harbour Drive, you see government notice boards. Much of the communication with the George Town people was done on these boards. Beside it was H. O. Merren's grocery and hardware store. On the left corner was Ethel Cook-Bodden's Yankee Notion Shoppe. The building next to it was the R. E. McTaggart & Brother store, and next to it was Merren's dry goods store. This corner was the centre of activity for Grand Cayman.

...and NOW

This is the most famous and most publicized scene in Grand Cayman. The Cayman Islands Museum, formerly the Old Courts Building, is headquarters for myriads of collected items of interest. Those interested in the island and her history should visit the museum.

A welcomed sight to the Cayman
people was the docking of the
Merco, a small ship owned by Mr.
H. O. Merren. It brought
passengers, goods and mail from
other ports.

Small ships and fishing boats were
regularly seen anchored off shore.
In early years the men who went
to sea were the major supporters
of the Grand Cayman economy.

The beach at North Side was not as inviting as Seven Mile Beach, primarily because of the rocky bottom near the shore. This photo was taken at a rather remote area. The ominous storm clouds were not frequently seen in this fashion on Grand Cayman.

Bill Compton and I persuaded several young boys to take us for a boat ride on Hog Sty Bay. During this short excursion I was able to take pictures of the George Town skyline.

A seaplane (converted Navy PBY) anchored in North Sound. The plane would usually stay overnight, leaving the following morning with passengers and mail bound for Tampa, Florida.

Previous pages:

The 1952 skyline of George Town was impressive for a Caribbean town situated on an island with no airstrip, no paved roads and a limited amount of transportation by sea. It stood as a testimonial to the industrious, progressive-minded residents of the island.

This photo was taken from South Church Street looking across the harbour where the *Caymania* is docked. Buildings in the background include the Customs Warehouse, Dr. Malley McTaggart's shop and Elmslie Memorial Church. George Town Primary School can be seen over the bow of the ship.

The thatched-covered Customs Building with the "waiting shelter" just behind it. A constable stands on the dock used by passengers going to and from the seaplane. A boat carried passengers to and from the plane, which was anchored a little off shore. Two airplane engines, salvaged from a sunken plane, lie behind the customs building. A seaplane went down in North Sound. It seems that the hatch was not securely fastened on takeoff, causing it to take on too much water and sink. The engines were deemed worth saving.

THEN...

The *Merco* is docked at George Town Harbour. In
addition to merchandise for the shops, the boat brought
needed items to Cayman families. They often secured
goods from mail-order houses in the U.S. Occasionally
an automobile would be on board.

...and NOW

What a contrast between 1952 and the present day. Here you see a large cargo ship being loaded or unloaded. The tremendous volume of goods and products from many countries of the world is truly amazing.

A beautiful sight — the seaplane resting at its mooring in North Sound. It was protected from the occasional rough waters of the open sea by the reefs that guarded the sound. The Cayman people were fortunate to have a large, protected area of water that was smooth enough most any time for a seaplane to take off or land.

The *Caymania* is docked in George Town Harbour. This was a very capable vessel that made countless trips to Cayman in all kinds of weather. She was owned by the J. S. Webster & Sons company. They were headquartered in Jamaica.

THEN...

An ideal day for a stroll down Harbour Drive in George Town. The cream-coloured building with brown trim on the left was the Customs Warehouse. The white building next to it was Dr. Malley McTaggart's shop. Beyond that, in the distance, was George Town Primary School. The bushes on right were in front of Miss Frances Bodden's house. Beside her house (not shown) was the old Bayview Hotel. On the right you can see the spire and a portion of Elmslie Memorial Church.

...and NOW

The casual stroll on the previous page has given way to the scene below. Harbour Drive is now a very busy street with an occasional traffic jam. Elmslie Memorial Church, in the centre of the picture, has remained to this day a landmark. The church was constructed in 1920. Queen Elizabeth, during her 1994 visit to Grand Cayman, attended a Sunday morning service there. Prince Philip, Duke of Edinburgh, read a Scripture passage from Romans (text 8:18-25) during the service.

This small Cayman building,
which had the same design as
many of the homes, housed the
Coroner's and the Clerk of Court's
offices. Through the years trials
were held at a number of places,
including the Old Courts Building
and the Town Hall. The lower part
of the sign out front was used to
communicate with the general
public.

This photo of the skyline was
taken from a little further out into
the harbour than the double-page
picture on pages 70 and 71. It
shows a few more of the buildings
along Harbour Drive and South
Church Street.

THEN...

A man riding a motorcycle on Shedden Road, going
away from the seawall on Harbour Drive. On the right is
H. O. Merren's grocery and hardware store. On the left,
at the corner, is Ethel Cook-Bodden's Yankee Notion
Shoppe. The two-story building next to it was the R. E.
McTaggart & Brother store. Next to it was Merren's dry
goods store. The small cloud of dust behind the
motorcycle was caused by the unpaved street.

...and NOW

This photo was taken as I stood near the seawall on Harbour Drive. The approaching automobiles are on Shedden Road. Although this presently seems to be the busiest corner on the island, the appearance has changed very little in the last half century. The buildings on either side of the corner, except for the one on the left, remain the same as in 1952. The building on the right (out of the picture) is now the Cayman Islands Museum and is one of the oldest buildings in the Cayman Islands.

THEN...

Bill Compton and Ertis Ebanks chat in front of the thatched-covered Customs Building on the shore of North Sound. The building was constructed in the 1940s.

...and NOW

The front entrance of the modern terminal at the airport on Grand Cayman, where many large jets land and take off each day, bringing thousands of visitors. It is also near North Sound.

THEN...

A beautiful, early morning shot of the *Caymania*. It was always a welcomed sight to the Cayman people. It meant passengers and needed goods had arrived. The *Caymania* was formerly a yacht owned by the Singer Sewing Machine Company. The J. S. Webster & Sons company purchased it for use as a cargo and passenger vessel.

...and NOW

Grand Cayman is a very popular stop for cruise ships. During a recent visit I saw four of these large vessels anchored in George Town Harbour at the same time. They bring multiplied thousands of visitors to the island each year.

THEN...

The Town Hall in George Town was a busy place. In addition to community meetings, some court sessions were held there. Very soon after Bill and I arrived, we attended one of the trials. A magistrate had come from Jamaica for the trial of an accused woman. It was built in 1923 by Captain Rayal Bodden as a court house and community assembly. The Clock Tower, built in honor of King George V, has stood in front of the Town Hall since 1937.

...and NOW

Like many of the older buildings of Grand Cayman, the Town Hall helps preserve the historic interest of this "island gem" in the Caribbean. The difference is that now it is nestled among busy traffic on paved streets, thousand of people walking on concrete sidewalks, and large, modern buildings. But, as you can see, the aging edifice is much the same as in 1952.

THEN...

The Post Office was a very important place to the Cayman people. After the arrival of the seaplane or one of the ships, it was buzzing with activity. Many of the Cayman men went to sea to make a living for their families; therefore, loved ones back home were anxious for news from ports around the world. The Post Office was the link between them and their loved ones. It was built in 1939 during the administration of Sir Allan Cardinall.

...and NOW

The Post Office in George Town
serves the whole of Cayman. It has
remained virtually unchanged
since it was built by Captain Rayal
Bodden. It originally served as a
government building with
treasury and customs offices and
a post office. It presently houses
2,000 postal boxes.

THEN...

A view from Shedden Road, looking toward the sea. On
the left is H. O. Merren and Company, which sold
millinery and footwear. Next to it was Merren's grocery
and hardware departments. Across the street was
Merren's dry goods department. Next to it was the R. E.
McTaggart & Brother store. Beyond that, on the corner,
was Ethel Cook-Bodden's Yankee Notion Shoppe.
Caymanians are enjoying a typical sunny day.

...and NOW

This photo shows that parts of Cayman — busy sections of George Town — remain much the same as in 1952, save for the crowds, the traffic and other modern trappings.

With sure hands and feet the Cayman men repaired the equipment. When the rope jammed someone had to go up and free it.

Pictured here are the twin sons of Rev. Hastings, pastor of the Church of God on Grand Cayman, with a playmate. Their toys were whatever they could find that seemed interesting.

Embarking on an Incredible Adventure

On June 6, 1952, Bill Compton and I boarded an Eastern Airlines plane in Chattanooga, Tennessee, bound for Tampa, Florida. The following day we joined several other passengers on a converted Navy PBY amphibian plane, destined for Grand Cayman.

As we took off from the runway in Tampa, little did we realize the exhilaration we would experience as the plane touched down on the reef-protected waters of North Sound. In the text and photographs of this book you have found my account of many more of our experiences. It is a joy to share them with you.

The enjoyment of most everything I ever possessed or experienced has been enhanced as I shared it with others. For that reason I have taken great pleasure in sharing the photographs and my reflections with the citizens of Grand Cayman and the multitudes of visitors who find their way to her shores each year.

Helping me to pass along my recollections and the pictures has been Marilyn, my wife of 44 years. I appreciate her help in arranging the sequence of the photos and valuable suggestions concerning the total manuscript. In the above photo Marilyn and I (I am the photographer) are enjoying a beautiful Cayman scene while at the home of Captain Charles and Carole Kirkconnell.

NOW...

Forty-seven years — nearly a half century — is a long time to watch the progress and growth of anything, especially an island — an island like Grand Cayman. But that's what I did. And the thing that made the observance more unusual is that I watched it from afar — from the United States, never setting foot on her shores during the first 42 years following my initial visit.

I often talked about the island and things I saw during that visit, and how they must be changed by now. I saw pictures in magazines and travel brochures and watched television news reports that showed her progress, but I didn't go back. Many times I thought about going back...to see the changes. I wanted to go back, but somehow never did.

Through those years my life in the U.S. was progressive and blessed. (The publishers have put a brief biographical sketch on the flap of the jacket for those who might be interested.)

In 1992 I was sitting in my office in Garland, Texas, a Dallas suburb, and came across a box of slides — photos that I had taken on that first visit. It had been about 40 years since I had looked at them. I knew the things shown on those slides had changed, but for some reason I wondered what they would look like in prints, so I proceeded to have them made. When I looked at the prints for the first time I immediately wanted to share them — especially with the Cayman people.

I soon was made aware that I had the most complete set of colour pictures, made before the building of the airstrip, in existence. I was encouraged to put them into a book — and now you have seen it.

As I said in my preface, I did go back, but I found that the Grand Cayman that I knew no longer exists — except in my memory...and in this book.

...and THEN

I jumped at the opportunity to make the trip to Grand Cayman with Bill Compton. I had completed only two years of my college training; therefore, I had not traveled a great deal. In fact I had never been out of the U.S., so this promised to be a trip of a lifetime. As I look back on it, it truly was. I don't know any young person who ever had such an experience, especially in 1952. The excitement and adventure that was mine has remained one of my most cherished memories.

I certainly was not an accomplished photographer , so to have my photographs published in a book of this nature is truly a thrilling continuation of my earlier adventure.

I can only wish that each person who reads the book will find it interesting and informative and will feel only a fraction of the thrill I enjoyed while on Grand Cayman in 1952.

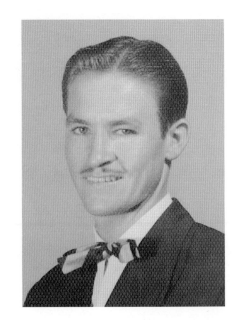